I0109091

A HEART IN MOTION

Celebrate freedom! Celebrate life!
Lacresha N. Hayes

A HEART IN MOTION

Celebrate freedom! Celebrate life!

Lacresha N. Hayes

LANICO MEDIA HOUSE
Arkansas•Texas•Louisiana

Copyright © 2014 by Lacresha Hayes. All rights reserved. No part of this book may be reproduced in any form or by any means, electronically or mechanically, including photocopying, without permission in writing from the author.

ISBN: 978-0-9886772-0-3

Unless otherwise noted, all Scripture quotations are from the King James Version of the Bible.

Cover photo: Larisa Koshkina

Publisher is Lanico Media House, an imprint of Lanico Enterprise, 13810 Greyfield Lane, Houston, Texas 77047.

Printed in the United States of America

No one can appreciate freedom like someone who was once bound. It takes on a whole new meaning. This book is for my mom, where all my poetry began. May she rest in Christ until we meet again.

INTRODUCTION

I've loved poetry since I was a child, when my mom would to fill my notebooks with long, soul-stirring poems. Artistic expression has been a lifesaver for me, helping me get through the many traumatic experiences I've had. This book, the third in my poetic journals, holds special meaning for me, primarily because I was able to shake off all the restrictions about what I should and should not write. I was able to fully express myself, my ideas, my faith, my fears and my fantasies.

The title for this book, *A Heart in Motion*, came from a conversation I had with a good friend, Celestine. Most of these poems were written while I was at the lowest point of my life, but even so, they reflect a genuine hope for better days. After finishing with my legal struggles, the first thing on my agenda was this book, hence the subtitle. Finally, I feel free in every area. That freedom has spilled over into my writing. I can hardly express how beneficial my writing skills have been in sharing my newfound freedom and wholeness.

A Heart in Motion is a book that I hope will inspire poetry lovers to live a life above the restrictions of small-minded naysayers and negative thinking. There are many lessons that this book can teach, the first of which is dealing with your own pain and those inner issues that hold you captive. For me, I did that through my spiritual relationship with God. The next lesson is dealing with the people and things in your life that hinder your growth, your process of becoming. The final lesson is embracing the fullness of who you are, flaws and all. This book is my way of celebrating me, of loving me deeply, passionately and fully.

I hope you will keep your heart open as you read. Let your heart go on this journey with me and maybe we can all celebrate freedom, life and inspiration together. Remember, it isn't where you've been, where you come from or what weaknesses you possess. What is important is where you're going. Poetry could be the vehicle to get you there. It was for me. Happy reading!

~

But God hath chosen the foolish things of the world to confound the wise; and God hath chosen the weak things of the world to confound the things which are mighty; And base things of the world, and things which are despised, hath God chosen, yea, and things which are not, to bring to nought things that are: That no flesh should glory in his presence.

1 Corinthians 1: 27-29

Highway of Hope

ONLY DAD I HAD

I tell you this because you are my dad
The only one I've ever had
And some of this will sound quite bad
Because for a long time I was my heart was sad

It's in your power to do anything but fail
This I know about you all too well
Yet it seems you turned your head
As my whole life was torn to a shred

You were my hope until I turned away
I felt like little more than lifeless clay
My heart was ravished with pain
I thought eventually I'd go insane
And my tears seemed to never dry
As I questioned you why, why, why
The more I tried, the worse things became
I was covered in guilt and shame

Because if even you didn't want me
What good would my life ever be
I even tried to convince myself you weren't real
To cover some of the emptiness I would feel

But, I'd seen enough to know you were there
Yet it wasn't enough to convince me you care
Oh I could preach it to sisters and brothers
Because I knew that you loved all the others

But I felt worthless, like a total reject
I couldn't grasp your love from any aspect
So I begged you to let me die
Attempt after attempt I would try
I got so desperate, I nearly self-destructed
All that you'd miraculously constructed
I cannot believe I could be so blind
But in the nick of time you opened my mind

Then you revealed the beauty of ME
Opened my eyes so I could see
All those wasted angry days I began to rue
As you made all things new

Your character was hard for me to embrace
Because I had yet to see your face
And since you didn't answer all of my tears
My heart had been filled with fears

I was seeking personal proof you could hear me
Constant assurance that you loved me
Trying to make you pay a debt you didn't owe
This realization was a heck of a blow

Because now it is terribly plain
You are not swayed by human pain
It is love that motors your will
Yielding to it means being faithfully still
No grappling or wrestling to get a rise out of you
But simply doing what we are told to do
The emotions of man is not your priority
They keep us walking contrary to your authority

But you, oh God, never stop being a dad

Never with our foolishness do you get so mad
That you walk away from all you've made
And forget the sacrifice you've already paid

I tell you this because I must repent
So much time wasted and spent
Forgive my arrogance, wash away my pride
Do spiritual surgery inside

Oh, my Father, my heart is glad
Because this foolish woman can call you dad
The only one I ever had
And you are the best, might I add

GOD HAS ONE WILL

God has one will
Only one path is real
All else is but illusion
No exception, no exclusion

God has one will
Not predicated upon how we feel
Determined before time began
Without the input of any man

God has one will
It comes when the heart is still
It is as final as the end
Not even with prayer will it bend

God has one will
One place we're meant to kneel
One Lord in whom we must trust
One answer for our lust

God's will is man's salvation
His sacrifices prove this revelation

I NEED

Grass needs the fall of rain
Rivers need the ocean
Bees need sweet flowers
Birds need the trees
But of all the needs I may mention
Only one keeps my attention

I need oxygen just to live
I need water, food and shelter
I may even need a friend or two
But there's nothing I need more than you

I need love on which to thrive
I need peace, joy and hope
Sometimes I feel the need to be new
But there's nothing I need more than you

I need knowledge to live in this world
I need wisdom, correction and understanding
And always I need what is true
What could be truer than you

WITHOUT YOU

I'm thirsty
My heart is panting
My sight is failing
My life dissipating

Oh how I need thee
Without you, there's no me

My soul is longing
There's no joy within
There's no hope
Nor do I have any peace

Oh how I need thee
Without you, there's no me

I'm crying out for more of you
Every fiber of me is yearning
All of me is in need
More of you lest I die

Oh how I need thee
Without you, there's no me

SEE HIS FACE

He sends help to the needy
Refuge to the homeless
Rest for the weary
Strength for the weak

Christ continues to plead our case
So that we may see his face

He's father to the fatherless
Friend to the lonely
A voice for the mute
Eyes for the blind

Christ continues to plead our case
So that we may see his face

HOPELESSLY WICKED

Hopelessly wicked
But desperate for You
Thirsting for a touch from You

Feeble at heart
Weakness of mind
But strong in my desire to find

Meaning in pain
Joy through rain
Smiles in sorrow
Hope in tomorrow

Hopelessly wicked
But desperate for You
I got to have a touch from You

ANXIETY

An endless hunger, a very dim light
A hole as dark as death gripping me tight

No satisfaction
No peace within
Seems no escape
From the jaws of sin

But I keep up the struggle
I continue to believe
All my ailments
God can relieve

I cannot fathom
Why the delay
It causes me grief
When I try to pray

The disappointment
I take it in stride
Remembering Jesus
And the reason He died

Though it hurts, I try not to cry
I remember
Upon whom I rely

MY STORY

Oh heart of mine, tell your story
You be humble and give God the glory

Man after man, yes I cared for them all
But time after time I continued to fall
Wound upon wound was given to me
Eventually leading me to the Light I needed to see

I searched for value through flawed men
Something like seeking safety in a lion's den
Foolishness was my bread, my bed was my back
Open legs made me a target for the enemy's attack

In the throes of disaster, I cried a river
I think of it now with a shiver
Full of pain, I lost my way
I'd get a good guy and still wouldn't stay

The void in me was deeper than a well
The neediness had me under a spell
Fear kept me running all day and night
But it was in vain since I had no sight

Many loved me the best they could
Even when I couldn't give it back as I should
But God showed me the road of honor and respect
Showed nothing but love for this reject

Then God filled the moon-sized craters of my heart
Removed every obstacle that kept us apart
Oh heart of mine, tell your story
You be humble and give God the glory

SLUMBER

Slumber, why must you evade
Awake endless hours I stayed
Until dream from reality I could not tell
And minutes sunk into a bottomless well

I see, now, myself in the hues of blue
Serenity, calm, peace as quiet as dew
I dance upon clouds that bounce like a ball
Then I jump off into a freefall

Somewhere at the end I shall close my eyes
And await the majestic, elusive sunrise
Refreshed and alive I shall rouse with glee
Because this Son has set me free

ANSWERS

Why should I fret the night away
Pacing the halls of my mind
Unsure of what the future holds
Nor are the answers easy to find

Why should I fear the unknown
Letting tomorrow rob me of today
Walking in the spirit of apprehension
It does no good anyway

I resolve now to trust God
Yielding my life to His plan
Not questioning and doubting
Nor seeking answers from mortal man

I resolve to have faith in His power
Choosing His eternal love
Rejecting all that come against it
Because He sent my answer from heaven above

DEEP STIRRING

A deep stirring rises from within
Here is my heart, would you rend
No more than whispered dreams
But my heart tears at the seams

A deep stirring rises from within
A desperate plea of one seeking to mend
Weary with the groans that express my plight
But there's a gathering for a bonfire tonight

A deep, deep stirring rises from within
All this grace and love available to lend
I thus choose this happy place
The only part of me to behold your face

Take now the dross as my heart is aflame
Purified gold is never the same
Burn ever deeper and always bright
May I always have the stirring I feel tonight

WE OWE IT TO YOU

Our capacity to grow
Our ability to see
Our desire to know
Our drive to be

We owe it all to you, Lord

All that we gain
The things we win
All the healing from pain
The peace you send

We owe it all to you, Lord

The cars we drive
Even the place we live
Each plateau at which we arrive
As well as the things we're able to give

We owe it all to you, oh Lord

FAILING FAITH

I want to be in faith
To live like I know you're there
I want to help those who struggle
Show them how much you care

I want to be a pillar
Someone others can call
I want to be steady and strong
Even when my back is against the wall

But the trials of my life
And the doubts in my mind
Combine to keep me unstable
And make my faith hard to find

Misplaced and neglected
My faith is failing fast
At the rate I'm going
I'm not sure how long I can last

I need you to come to my aid
I need to hear you speak
I need your guidance
For I have grown weak

I do want to be in faith
Because I'm sure you're there

And even while it's failing
I know for sure you do care

At the end of my rope
I continue to reach out
With only a mustard seed of faith
Warring against endless doubt

Still, you promised
You said it only takes a little
Thus I stand on your Word
It won't fail, not one jot or one tittle

Journey of Emotions

NOW ALONE

Sweet lover, dear heart
You promised we'd never part
But never at all did you say
Sometimes things won't go our way

There was a time your grip was strong
You'd hold me in your arms all night long
You helped me through every fear
Except the one of not having you here

My best friend, companion ever
Charming, loving, witty, clever
A spouse upon which I came to depend
Yet our dream came to a sudden end

Oh my sweetness, I'm so alone
How do I cope with you being gone
So many things I never said
Many of your signals went unread

My only comfort is the life you led
Kindness and love from the day we wed
Your faithfulness to God and patience with me
How you lived stress and worry free

But I know that death isn't the end
It's an avenue to begin again
So into the arms of God I release you
But never shall I stop loving you

DOOR NUMBER TWO

It's a trap behind door number two
It's a disaster there waiting for you
The "what might have been" is a lie
Let me explain the reason why

Just as no one can undo the past
No one can say what will last
He may promise he'll never stray
But he doesn't know what's coming his way

He may make more money with his brain power
But he cannot predict his next hour
And he may even cater to you on bended knees
Trying to prove he aims to please

You don't know 10 years up the road
This new guy is a bomb preparing to explode
But the man you have now in your bed
You once judged as good enough to wed

Any other door leads to sinking sand
Because another has already taken your hand
The showcase is not for the married gal
Bopping Betty, Sue or Trina is not your pal

Marriage isn't Burger King to have your way
It was created for us to stick and stay
Don't fall into the trap behind door number two
It may be the death of you

TODAY WILL MARK THE END

I came to a conclusion today
I took some time to think and pray
You said you want to go your own way
And maybe you'll be back one day
So now I choose to back away
This is a game I won't play
It doesn't matter what I say
I know I cannot convince you to stay

Thus today will mark the end
All the ties that bind us we will rend
My original plans I now amend
I open my heart and release you, my friend

All the vows that we swore
The love we had, the relationship I used to adore
It was not enough to heal the core
And always you were seeking for more
Ever my heart your actions tore
Seemed pain was all we had in store
We couldn't get up from the floor
And shame was the coat we wore

But today will mark the end
All the ties that bind we will rend
Original plans we must amend
I open my heart and release you, my friend

IT'S TOO LATE

I was your woman
I was your best friend
I stood by your side
I was there until the end

I was your backbone
Always holding up your slack
I never abandoned you
I always had your back

But you walked away
You left me alone
You went on with your life
And now I've moved on

Things began to break down
So you called me last night
Now you want to come back to me
You think we'll be alright

But baby it's too late
Honey it's too bad
You lost the best thing you've ever had

IT'S TOO BAD

It's been less than a year
And your life is full of trouble
The person you thought would hold you down
Left you drowning in the rubble

It all sounds good in the beginning
When promises are abundant as rain
But when the real problems came
She left you doubled over in pain

Now your eyes have opened
And you see what you really had
You want to turn back the hands of time
But baby, it's too bad

Now you want my love back
You call sounding all sad
You think an apology will suffice
But baby, it's too bad

FOOLISH GIRL

I believed your lies
And heeded your calls
But that was my demise
The most humiliating of all my falls

I tended to your needs
Served you like you were a king
Took time to sow good seeds
Tried to give you everything

Many days I cried alone
Not sure which way to go
We'd fuss and yell over the phone
What would set you off, I didn't know

I was a foolish girl with dreams
Looking for something you didn't possess
Falling apart at the seams
Feeling the pain of the press

Look at all you've done to me
The fights, the deception, the pain
You put my life in jeopardy
Left me standing uncovered in the rain

My life took a dangerous turn
I did things I knew I shouldn't

Everyone was telling me to let you go
But for a long time, I just couldn't

Foolishness upon foolishness
Until I began to pray
Slowly but surely
God sent the light my way

I was a foolish girl
I put my hopes in a man
Tried to make you the one
But it wasn't God's plan

I've wised up these days
I no longer play with my life
I've learned to keep my gems
Until a real man makes me his wife

CHALLENGE OF LOVING YOU

I received a challenge today
Could I accept you in every way
Could I stay with you come what may
Could I be patient as I pray

Could I believe the words you say
Could I continue to send other men away
Could I stand with you another day
Could I find a reason to stay

Could I ignore the games you play
Could I forgive every time you stray
Could I keep my anger at bay
Could I love you until our hair turns gray

I received a challenge today
I saw the cost that I'd have to pay
All I can do now is have faith and pray
That through it all, God will have His way

NOT JUST YET

I'm not quite ready yet
There's so much left to be done
Though I've accomplished a lot
There's more battles left to be won

Quitting time is not right now
My best days are still ahead
As the years pass, I'll get better
I'll follow where I'm led

Death called for me
Invited me into the deep
Not just yet am I ready for that
This life is mine a little longer to keep

There are people in the world
They are waiting on me
They need to hear the message
My testimony they must see

Not just yet, death
My master isn't finished here
Many more miles left to run
A few hurdles left to clear

I CELEBRATE

I celebrate my freedom
I give God all the praise
No more chains bind me
My head and hands I raise

I celebrate my miracle
It was only through God's power
When I felt helpless
God was my strong tower

I celebrate my restoration
God healed my backslidden ways
He raised me up from the muck
Then He lengthened my days

I celebrate my relationship
My heavenly Father calls me by name
He placed his seal upon my heart
Throughout eternity staking his claim

Leap of Love

LOVE ANEW

When I first met you
I was full of desire
Songs and poetry
Our love would inspire

But soon the bad overshadowed the good
Things stopped working as they should
For a brief moment, I lost sight
Of all the things we had that was right

Though it seemed bad was all I could see
I knew there was no other man in the world for me
Always I didn't show my appreciation
Because my heart was filled with reservations

Still I'm so glad you found the strength to stay
And that I have the pleasure of standing here today
Declaring again my love anew
Honoring, admiring and adoring you

Yes, when I first met you
I was full of desire
Now that I know you
My soul is afire
Songs and poetry our love would inspire
The heat between us can make an Eskimo perspire
There's no man above you I admire
And of you, honey, I will never tire

LOVE YOU RIGHT

Baby, sweet baby, I need you tonight
I don't want to fuss or fight
I just want to love you right

I want you to wrap me up in your arms
I want to partake of your charms
I want to taste you because you're so sweet
I want to bask in your heat

I want to kiss all over your chest
As you feel the swell of my breast
Now trace my curves with the palm of your hand
Hug, caress, kiss, tantalize me and

When my heart begins to pound
I want to wrap my legs around
Your body, pulling us face to face
Letting your passion set the pace

I want you completely nude
Your beautiful body keeps me in the mood
And no, this time no speaking in code
I want to love you until you explode

Give it your all, no holding back
Love me until the sky turns black

I'm not a booty call, I'm your wife
Love me like you need me in your life

Look at every inch of me
Commit my body to memory
Let the sound of my voice assure you
That all of me wants all of you

Baby, sweet baby, I need you tonight
I don't want to fuss or fight
I just want to love you right

UNCOMFORTABLE ATTRACTION

You make me feel a million things
Being with you is like soaring on wings
But sometimes I can't read you well
If you're happy or not, I can't tell

There's no one else with whom I'd spend my days
You mesmerize me in so many ways
But our downs feel extraordinarily low
How to keep you close to me, I don't know

When I think for sure you love me true
The game of life throws us something new
But even in the bad, I always stay
I promised you I wouldn't go away

While uncomfortable I surely am now
I will get over it somehow
Because this attraction shall ever be
Fire, ice and lightning between you and me

JEALOUSY

Just like a supervisor
You're always looking over my shoulder
You don't trust me at all
Day by day, you get colder

You watch my every move
You monitor my phone
You verify everything I say
You never want me to be alone

No doubt it's your own indiscretions
That fuel your jealous rages
You know the treatment you deserve
Same story throughout the ages

You threaten me daily
But violence will get you nowhere
I respond to love, patience and kindness
Spend time showing me that you care

It's your jealousy tearing us apart
It's your fear that is breaking your heart

WHAT MAKES A MARRIAGE

Without love, it is but ceremony
Without loyalty, it is empty words
Without patience, it is a void hope
Without faith, it is meaningless

Not with parades, recessionals and dances
Not even with the invitation of greatness
Not with the most lavish settings
Not with the inclusion of many rites

What makes a marriage isn't rituals
What makes a marriage isn't planning
What makes a marriage isn't a wedding
What makes a marriage isn't even a ring

It is the virtues of life that must combine
Two separate souls must intertwine
They must stay connected to the Vine
To make a marriage truly divine

LOST IN YOU

I'm with you everyday
Watching you make your own way
Seeing your issues and the struggle
The things you are required to juggle

I listen every time you tell your story
Reliving and learning about your days of glory
I watch the things that lighten your eyes
Listen for the stuff that gives you a rise

Of your idiosyncrasies I am aware
But love you forever, I just might dare
Looking at what others go through
I choose us and I'm lost in you

You have a tenderness that melts my heart
You're nutty and amusing, but you're also smart
This is why I'm so lost in you
It's who you are, not just the things you do

DESPERADO

Love's desperado
Come riding in on your horse
Take me away, let's change the course
Glide in through the air
Just come if you dare

Rebel with a cause
Come win my love
Woo and pursue me
Only do not abuse me

Outlaw of romance
Please give us a chance
Place your hands here
Put your lips there
I'll teach you how to love me
I'll show you how to share

My desperado
Loving you is criminal
But tis true I'm addicted
To this heart wound you've inflicted

YOUR FAITH

Follow your faith and not your eyes
Open your heart and realize
This should come as no surprise
Carnal sight can lead to your demise

There's no time like today
To allow the Lord to have His way
To pledge that you will never stray
And make the most of this day

But you must not doubt His love or will
Because fear your faith will always kill
And we don't live by how we feel
But by the Spirit which is our seal

So now, Father, as a couple we seek your face
Desiring to sit in that holy place
Asking strength to run this race
Thanking Jesus for pleading our case
Amen

SPYGAMES

Verify the details
Information truly expels
All reasons for my doubt
The games I can do without

Prove what you say
Don't leave me in disarray
Then I'll know for sure
That what we have is pure

I don't want to go through your phone
I want to leave the spy games alone
But every sneaky thing you do
Makes me further distrust you

This fear isn't what I want to feel
I would like our relationship to heal
But I cannot ignore the facts
And you obviously cannot conceal your acts
So here we are playing spy games

CONTRADICTIONS

Life is too short
But it can feel so long
Opportunity knocks only once
But before you can open, it has gone

Don't put off for tomorrow what's for today
Because tomorrow never comes
Yet we age from day to day
Faster than a river runs

This world is filled with contraindications
Deceiving even God's best
And if with truth you may still be deceived
God have mercy on the rest

So though I'm angry I come in peace
Though it seems a contradiction
All this anger I release
Along with any prior convictions
I will not let our togetherness die at the hand of
contradictions

MY SWEET LOVE

I love to see him smile
My heart beats with his grin
My eyes are full of him
I've lost sight of other men

I try to tell him I love him
Show him what I feel inside
So desperate to connect with him
I've set aside my pride

I can see right through him
I know he's really not so tough
He's just very cautious
He's been hurt and disillusioned enough

But each time he laughs
My purpose becomes clear
I want to make sure it stays that way
I want to get him past his fear

He's my sweet love
I'll never cause him anguish or pain
I'll never take anything from him
I seek only his gain

BETTER THAN SUNRISE

I didn't suspect it
You caught me by surprise
Your love is better than a sunrise

Tenderness and sensitivity
If only they knew
Every woman in the world would be in love with you

Patience and selflessness
Occasionally demanding
In my opinion, you're simply outstanding

You're my sweet lover
Thoughtful and kind
The things you do blow my mind

I'm in love
I feel like singing a song
While lying in your arms all night long

I didn't suspect it
You caught me by surprise
Your love is better than a sunrise

WHEN YOU KNOW

On my mind all day long
Life feels like a love song
Missing you before you leave
Whatever you say I will believe

Can't stay angry even a little while
It disappears at the sight of your smile
Can't wait another minute to wear your ring
For you, I'll do almost anything

I have no problem following you
Doing what you ask me to
Treating you like my king
Yielding to you in everything

At this point is when you know
Just how far I'm willing to go
To hold on to this love I've sought for
There's nothing in life I want more

AFRAID OF LOVE

Once upon a time I was afraid of love
If it didn't come softly on the wings of a dove

Looking out amongst the people
All I see is grief
I perceive all the brokenness
People searching for relief

Men who cannot be trusted
They lie daily to their wives
Women with treacherous hearts
Living double lives

Divorces are prominent
Thousands by the day
Few reconciliations
Everyone wants their own way

Gone are the days of compromise
Gone are the days of respect
Gone are the days of wooing
There's nothing left to expect

It's not easy to love these days
The chances of pain are great
But in the end it is worth it
If you find the right mate

TO COMMUNICATE

To speak is a true gem
To hear is a blessing from Him
But to listen is a gift
Your soul it will uplift

Communication is the key
It shows love between you and me
And when you hear what I say
It changes the course of our day

You may not always want to hear it
But, if you will endure it
You will prove that you care
About all the things I want to share

When you cut me off while I speak
You make me feel unwanted or weak
But when you make a sacrifice to hear
It makes me want to draw near

I listen so I can witness your life
That's my duty as a wife
It shows that you are important to me
And my priorities are where they should be

It costs nothing to communicate
Do it now before it's too late

WISTFUL EXPRESSIONS

Wistful expressions of you
Don't they turn my brown eyes blue

So witty, a real charmer
Full of smarts, light and humor
Tongue as sharp as a whip
Eyes that pierce like a sword

Wistful expressions of you
Don't they turn my brown eyes blue

Blissful nights in your arms
But long days away from home
A paramour with class
Gallant wooer of my heart

Just wistful expressions of you
They always turn my brown eyes blue

FOR YOU

There's somebody for everybody
But not just anybody can touch this body
That's just for you

Everyone needs someone
And for me you are that one
I'm reserved just for you

I went from nothing to everything
Because you chose to give me your ring
Always, all of this is for you

I called and you answered every time
You brought rhythm to my rhyme
I'm the end of the rainbow, for you

SIGN OF THE TIMES

Romantic connections
Haphazardly made
Dangerous games
Casually played

Signs of the times
Constantly ignored
Forbidden territory
Recklessly explored

Sexual inhibitions
Now released into the air
Partner after partner
Without so much as a care

Signs of the times
And impending doom
The loss of our women
The welcoming of gloom

COLORS OF LOVE

This is the fantasy of a queen
I don't mean to be obscene
But I'll bet you anything
In the end, you'll be my king

On that first, fabulous, surreal night
Our love color will be the purest white
And we will hold each other tight
As we ascend to a new height

Ecstasy will describe night number two
When I'll have you decked in blue
The pleasure you experience will be new
The lengths of my imagination, you haven't a clue

On the third night, I'll be in red
I'll meet you in the middle of the bed
My kisses will start with your head
My lips will go wherever they're led

Our fourth night is all about black
The color of power getting us on track
There won't be a place from front to back
Nothing unloved, not a spot or crack

On our last night, purple will robe you, my king
I'll yield to you in everything

All of me I will bring
Because I'm the one who wears your ring

This is the fantasy of your queen
Baby, I'm not being obscene
Just trying to show you what you mean
And enjoying this new love that's fresh like green

DARK EYES

Eyes as dark as a starless night
As captivating as a tidal wave
There's not even a hint of light
And they are as hungry as the grave

What do I love about my dark king
I could sum it up as everything
From head to toe, you're a beautiful man
And I'll always be your number 1 fan

But the depth of my ardent affection
Is only but a beautiful reflection
Of the glorious and resplendent sunrise
That hits my heart when I see your eyes

In the mystical darkness that flows from you
It is in your eyes I find what is true
That I can tour what's inside
See even the dreams that have already died

And in the planes and angles that is your face
Of many things there isn't a trace
But the lamp to your soul tells your story
Because this is where you'll get your glory

Royal one, precious, lovely altogether
I give you my heart as shelter from the weather

Of love and support, I give you an unlimited supply
I want to be the one upon whom you can rely

I want to wrap you up in the purest white
For all the darkness to become bright
I want you to have the chance to heal
So you won't miss something so fervid and real

The depth of my ardent affection
Is only but a beautiful reflection
And I would die a thousand deaths
Just to give you a few extra breaths

Path of Peace

ORDINARY?

Ordinary, plain, unremarkable me
Was living my life in uncertainty
Was afraid to reach for the moon
Because those big things are gone too soon

I cannot fathom what lies in the deep
Cannot even understand the wonder of sleep
I have yet to fully comprehend gravity
I'm just lil ole plain and simple me

It isn't me to cure the world's ills
I can barely discern how someone else feels
I can't bend steel, turn invisible or fly
Yet each day I have the power to hold my head high

You see, as ordinary and plain as I seem to be
Never will there be another me
I am exactly who I'm supposed to be
This is the revelation that set me free

PEOPLE AREN'T PERFECT

My lover has failed me
How could this be
But people aren't perfect
This I must see

Amazingly, I cannot be mad
And even though my heart is sad
People aren't perfect
Of this knowledge, I am glad

I won't let this break my stride
I'll do all my work on the inside
Because people aren't perfect
Including me and my pride

ACCEPT IT

I accept it
I heard you
It's a done deal
We're through

No more love
Too many tears
Too much bad
Throughout too many years

I accept it
You aren't mine
At first it hurt
But now I'm just fine

I have peace
I have faith and hope
The pain is over
I've learned to cope

ENLARGE MY HEART

Enlarge my heart's capacity
To live with the flaws of others
To see the beauty in them
To understand the purpose of grace
To willingly bestow mercy
To quickly forgive trespasses
To impart what virtues you've given me
To patiently learn from others
To never judge others harshly
To defend those who are defenseless
To speak for the muted ones
To lend my eyes to the blind

Father, enlarge my heart's capacity
To truly love all you've created
Enlarge my heart's capacity
Because to them all I am related

HEAL OUR MOUTHS

Heal our mouths, oh Lord
Tame these tongues
Sooth the mind that curses
And quench every fiery word arrow

Bloody, we're bloody
We kill with a sword
We speak evil against others
We mock and we lie

We do it from the pulpit
We do it from the pew
We do it with family
We even indulge with friends

It is our words that condemn us
It is our mouths that crucify
It is our tongues that pierce
Heal our mouths, oh Lord

SENSATIONS

The warmth of his hand
Meets the small of my back
The softness of his lips
Caress and tantalize my neck
His eyes light a blaze in my soul
His voice feeds the flames of my passion

Those same hands occasionally caress another
And my heart shatters at the thought
Because when I lie in his arms
All of the world and time seems to fade
And for a moment I forget the betrayal
And remember only the gentleness of his tone

My dignity fought with my affection
Dignity took a nosedive
Because each time he apologizes, I forgive him
Each lie he spews forth, I devour
Whatever he gives me I accept it
Because I'm caught up in all these sensations

His warmth, his coolness
His gentleness, his wrath
His sweetness, his cruelty
His genius, his insanity
I love the duplicity of the man
I guess, really, I simply love him

LOVE MUST BE

Love has no price sticker
Because the cost is too high
It cannot be purchased with money
Nor can it be leased or rented

Love can't be bargained for
And is not awarded to great debaters
No purpose under heaven is without it
And no person exempt from the desire for it

Love can't be stolen
Nor can cunning craftiness win it
No great or small actions can merit it
Love must be given

Love must be given because it costs everything
Love must be given because no one can afford it
Love must be given because no one deserves it
Love must be given because everyone needs it

Love is eternal, patient and true
Love is kind, gentle and tender
Love is powerful, but possesses a delicate touch
Love is God because God said He is Love

I SURVIVED

You thought you had the best of me
Thought that you'd break me
Thought I couldn't live without you
Thought I'd crash and burn without you
But I survived

You deserted me at my lowest point
While my life was out of joint
I didn't have a thing to my name
Yet you walked away all the same
But I survived

Our break up came at a high cost
For a brief period I felt completely lost
Wasn't sure if I could make it
All the pain, I couldn't take it
But I survived

Now I know what I'm made of
I understand the power of God's love
I can now stand alone
Because I know that I'm never on my own
Sweetheart, I survived

THE EFFECT

My heart melted
Rivers of rose petals flowed from within
This is the effect you have on me, my friend

Totally inspired
You've become my muse
And it's from you I take my cues

Daily I wait
Anxious to see your face
To witness how you move with grace

My heart has melted
Rivers of rose petals flowed from within
This is the effect you have on me, my friend

BEGINNING AND END OF US

I saw the beginning and the end of us
It was last night in my dream
We began like a raging river
Ended like a trickling stream

We enjoyed sweet companionship
And reveled in the excitement of it all
The passion and intimacy was mind-blowing
At first our problems seemed so small

We shared our secrets and our fears
We could totally trust one another
Even the doubts that we had
Were not hidden from each other

You were enough for me
And more than I could ever desire
But your family ties and commitments
Kept you at bay as I began to tire

Yet I believe in love upon first sight
And I know my dream was real
Because even seeing you walk away
Doesn't change how I feel

I saw the beginning and the end of us
But darling, I know it's never too late

To say all the things that should be said
And possibly change our fate

So now I take the first step
Welcome to my heart
What happens next is all on you
You can have it whole or only a part

The beginning has happened
The dream was true
But the end is up to us
It's about what we do

ANNOYED

Annoyed with this part of life
Not exactly what I expected
Annoyed with the people in it
Feel so disrespected

Annoyed with my station
Never wanted to see this place
Annoyed that history repeats itself
Same stuff right back in my face

Annoyed with the meddling
People can be so nosy
I guess they hadn't noticed I'm grown
Mess up my life while they come out rosy

Ugh, so annoyed
I just don't understand it
It all makes me sick
I can hardly stand it

THE SKILL

There's a rare skill I happen to possess
The ability to make strong men obsess
And lose themselves in curiosity
Greeting other suitors with animosity

Seems their lives are never the same
Once they feel the heat of my flame
And all of them say the exact same thing
"Baby, will you wear my ring?"

Now you may wonder about what I say
What's the source of this sway
It isn't my beauty else it wouldn't be rare
But I'll explain just to be fair

I let men be who they are
And if my man isn't up to par
I speak to the king who lives inside
And never do I attack his pride

God taught me something I stand by
Women of God, give it a try
What you want to grow, you must feed
Give tender words to nourish the seed

Forgive quite quickly then forget it all
Slowly he'll begin to let down his wall

Your kindness will give him wings to soar
And you will be the one he ever adore

Men are curious about what lies just out of reach
And ladies I don't mean to preach
But before your sex, he should know your mind
He should see your character before your grind

I know the behavior that's the common trend
But all that'll get you is a sex friend
Now if you want a man who'll be your mate
Speak to the king until that ruler becomes great

Show your king the depth of his reign
Set his heart free from every chain
Humble yourself and show your devotion
Set the plan of God in motion

SIMPLE LITTLE KISS

It was just a simple little kiss
But it turned my misery into bliss
The brushing of lips like a feather
But since that day we've been together

I remember the first day I made you blush
The day I told you I have a crush
Seeing you smile was so divine
There was a tingle down my spine

I wanted so badly just to touch
The face I'd come to admire so much
When I thought another second I couldn't wait
I had myself in a terrible state

It was then you gave me those lips
Sent my mind and body on trips
Then you used your fingers to trace
Slow, smooth lines to contour my face

In an instant again your mouth found mine
And I knew that we had crossed the line
I was so enraptured that I swore
Both my feet left the floor

It felt so good I thought I could fly
But I was so scared I wanted to cry

I felt hope cover all my pain
As the words you whispered numbed my brain

Seems your lips left a brand
I wish you could understand
It was like everything in life I had missed
Was supplied on the day we first kissed

In only seconds, all was rearranged
On a deep, emotional level, I was changed
It was just a simple little kiss
But it turned my misery into bliss

ARMS OF INSPIRATION

When I found you, I found arms of inspiration
Found a heart full of dedication
Found life without expiration
And you are now my motivation

In your arms, I feel at home
There's no reason for me to roam
No one else to capture my attention
I don't even have an honorable mention

There's only me and you
And this life to help each other through
We are witnesses for one another
Each vouching for the worth of the other

I know that I have your shoulders
Stronger than the oldest boulders
And baby you have all my loyalty
My promise to treat you as royalty

When I found you, I found arms of inspiration
And you are now my motivation

A GLANCE

You don't have to understand me
But give me a chance
There's a lot more to me
I deserve more than a glance

Beautiful, sophisticated, dangerously smart
Gentle, kind, yet sometimes impatient at heart
Full of love that I've yet to share
I care more than most others would dare

Haunted by some happenings of the past
But fully committed to making us last
Oppressed by a rage that lies inside
But determined to get rid of all my pride

The enigma you see
Often captivates even me
Yet I try to explain
Both my joy and my pain

You don't have to understand me
But give me a chance
There's a lot more to me
I deserve more than just a glance

THIS, MY DARLING, IS GOODBYE

The challenge that I see with you in my life
Has nothing to do with being your wife
It has more to do with the pain of the past
And how hard we've fought to make it last

Not that what we have isn't worth fighting for
But after giving it our all, it still requires more
Oh, my husband, I am saying goodbye
There's no sense in us living a lie

You're a sweet and wonderful person at heart
But our differences have torn us apart
We left our love unprotected
And lost touch with all we respected

Nevertheless, hopefully a friendship will remain
And in time, there'll be no more pain
Maybe one day we'll smile about it all
Because we'll have both found our call

This is the end but also a new beginning
It may feel like losing but we're actually winning
I will love you forever and a day and a spell
But I still must bid thee farewell

This, my darling, is goodbye!

SEE THROUGH YOU

I know you think I can't see through you
But the motives of your heart shine through
I see your doubts, uncertainties and fears
Late at night, I can feel your tears

You want a life unlike that of those you see
And you feel like the ticket to that is me
You want to be a good husband and a great man
But sometimes your mind is contrary to your plan

Two parts good guy and one part thug
Sometimes humble and sometimes smug
Still don't know who you were created to be
Or what in the world attracted me

God sent me to show you life above the norm
For you to experience peace despite the storm
To calm your nerves and show you a new way
To usher you into a new day

To give you my strength from deep inside
And to learn to love without all the pride
Together, we will live, learn and grow
Whatever else may come, I don't know

LACRESHA

Lasting impressions of the night before
Always excited when you walk through the door
Constant reminders of that special night
How you held me in your arms so tight
Excellent lover, my special friend
Still desiring you until the end
Having aftershocks from your touch
At last, I've found what I wanted so much

NICOLE

Never had someone so true
In love absolutely with you
Completely enraptured with the things you do
On another level, I'm someplace new
Leaving your essence behind like dew
Experiencing something reserved for very few

PUGH

Patrick, you make my heart skip a beat
Unquestionably, you knock me off my feet
Giving me good love and loads of joy
I feel like a kid with a brand new toy

WOUNDED WIFE

I was a wounded wife
The distress nearly ruined my life
Seems I couldn't avoid the strife
The pain cut through me like a knife

First came the broken promises and lies
I didn't heed the words of the wise
Then came the careless treatment
Too much time alone I spent

I was wounded by his flirtatious ways
How he chose to spend the majority of his days
Left seeking love from the wrong places
Losing definition between the two faces

I was wounded by his pride
He never once welcomed me inside
He loved me from a long handled spoon
Seems our love was over too soon

I was a wounded wife
God had to remove the strife
His grace was like a surgeon's knife
I thank Him for restoring my life

CONTRAST

I found myself drawn to the light
And now must bury an old woman tonight

She was nothing at all like me
We were as different as can be
She was the woman who seemed never to care
She did whatever she would dare

She never thought about consequences
She needed the light to bring her to her senses
She always had her pick of men
Her life was filled with each kind sin

She was arrogant with a hard head
She didn't know that she was the walking dead
But the light intervened in her mind
God had mercy because she was blind

He reanimated her lifeless clay
Gave her the gift called today
The life that exists now is mine
Living specifically for the divine

Humble, submissive, living obediently
Following God expediently
That old lady had me on the wrong road
Had me operating in hell mode

But this new person God created
Makes me feel completely elated
Into the darkness came His light
He robed me in heavenly white

All I can do now is compare and contrast
The life that is and the one from the past

POETRY IN MOTION

Poetry in motion
He makes my heart melt
All the emotions inside
Stronger than I ever felt

In love with his smile
Love the sound of his voice
Enjoy probing his mind
He's definitely my choice

But he's dangerous
And I have a little fear
Yet it dissipates quickly
When he holds me near

Poetry in motion
In him there is nothing phony
He moves like wisdom
He's a walking testimony

QUESTIONING

I can't stop thinking about you
You're always on my mind
Not sure how I feel about you
It's like walking around blind

One part of me adores you
All the quirky details included
Another part of me fears you
And that feeling can't be eluded

I'm not sure we fit
So many differences at heart
But you have charm and wit
You're sweet, thoughtful and smart

Baby, you give me the blues
But in the next breath you make me high
I keep searching your eyes for more clues
Not letting even a spark get by

This time isn't like those in the past
We both have more to give
I believe this relationship can last
And enrich these lives we live

NO TRUST

There's no trust
How can there be love
There's no true bond
Nothing worth speaking of

He does what he wants
Never considers how I feel
Hangs out with other women
But says my fears aren't real

There's no trust
How can our relationship survive
Yet I still desire him
He makes me feel alive

But there's no trust
And I honestly regret
All the things that keep happening
The stuff that keeps me upset

I've invested so much time
And I love him in spite
I never want to lose him
I want only to make it right

THE COMEBACK

We often make mistakes and fall short
Things we planned we have to abort
At times we find ourselves hopelessly behind
We're uptight and on edge with no peace of mind

But prayer has a purpose that's full of power
It can be initiated at any hour
God has His ear tuned in to hear
The cries of our hearts so He can pull us near

He molds and refashions the heart
His tapestry work is like pure art
And when all of His work is done
He places a banner over us that says we won

I've had it all and lost my way
From sound doctrine I began to stray
But God illuminated every area that was black
And orchestrated an amazing comeback

EXPRESSIONS

From my heart pours forth emotion
But I don't always know how to express it
I'm filled with love, hate, doubt and faith
The bad, I can't suppress it

Some days I feel like singing
Want to go skipping through fields of joy
Other days I want to be alone
I'm withdrawn, nostalgic, and sometimes even coy

Sometimes, I cry for no reason at all
Not sure if for happiness or pain
Sometimes I want to bask in the sunshine
Other times I long for the rain

Some nights I long for companionship
Some nights I want to be solo
Times when I want to be ignorant
Times I want to be in the know

I can't always explain myself
I'm an enigma even to me
But poetry has helped a lot
These poetic expressions set me free

EPILOGUE

There's a stereotype that exists and prevails. Many say artistic types are often misunderstood. I can't attest to this for everyone, but for me, it has often rung true. I think it is because of my poker face. It's almost flawless. People cannot seem to discern the strong undercurrent, the riptide that exists right under the surface.

The beauty of poetry and song is the expression of emotion and pent up energy. Words released from the soul ministers to the soul. Poetry should be the language of the soul because it is freedom that doesn't exist in any other area that I've found.

Most of my life, I felt alone, whether there were people around or not. I didn't have a companion of my soul, no one I could share the inner self with. But soon, my writing became my friend and while I wouldn't consider myself a Robert Frost or Maya Angelou, I know that I am a lover of words. I adore poetry. I appreciate the role it has played in my life and in my healing from the many horrible happenings of my past. It has also helped me celebrate life, love and liberty.

This book has been about sharing openly the sum of who and what I am. I'm not just a Christian, but I'm also a woman, a mother, a lover, a friend, a daughter, a sister, a business owner and a student of life. I'm a believer, but sometimes I doubt. I'm a lover but there are some things I hate. I'm human but living a spiritual, supernatural life. This book is about my human expression without the care of political correctness or the expectations of others. This is my third poetry book, the one that let's my hair down, so to speak.

A Heart in Motion is a fiesta, a book that I hope becomes a favorite for you. I hope that you found the rhythm of your life through this book, words that captured the essence of who you are, where you've been and where you're going. After all, this life is a journey and we're all on our way to some destination. Our hearts are ever evolving, growing, sometimes shrinking, but ever changing. Until the next time...

www.ingramcontent.com/pod-product-compliance
Lightning Source LLC
Chambersburg PA
CBHW062017040426
42447CB00010B/2030